A souvenir guide

# Moseley Old Hall

## Wolverhampton

GW00578057

**National Trust**

# A Home that Saved a King

# At first glance Moseley Old Hall appears to be a charming but perhaps unremarkable house.

The warm brick exterior and modest grounds have been slowly enclosed on all sides by the outside world. The motorway thunders close by, and the ever-expanding city of Wolverhampton has steadily made its way closer to this once secluded spot. This peaceful site feels under siege.

Yet Moseley Old Hall has seen off far worse; for two days in September 1651 this home was witness to events of such high drama – and such national significance – that over 350 years later they are still remembered. It played its part in one of the most exciting episodes in English history; it helped to save a king.

## The turning point
In 1651, England was in the last throes of the English Civil War. Charles I had been executed in 1649 and Cromwell's Rump Parliament had declared England a Commonwealth. Roman Catholics and Royalists found themselves persecuted, defeated and, in many cases, executed.

The Battle of Worcester on 3 September 1651 was a disaster for Royalist forces fighting for the heir to the crown, Charles II. With the town surrounded by Parliamentarian militia, and Cromwell's New Model Army at its core, Charles faced forces almost twice the size of his own. The resulting fight saw his army devastated. Accounts of the time describe a battlefield awash with blood, the young King fleeing the city through the only gate left open, St Martins. The Parliamentarians were hard on his heels,

but Charles had no plan, no idea where to go. He headed north but found his way blocked at every turn. For six weeks, the desperate Charles relied on a network of Royalist and Roman Catholic families for help, hiding in priest holes, barns and even trees, before finally heading for the south coast and the boat that would take him to safety in France.

Moseley Old Hall was the turning point in Charles's time on the run. The two, tense nights he spent hiding here gave the fugitive monarch and his allies enough time to form the basis of a plan, which would change many times, before his final escape to France. Today, its open fires, oak-panelled interior and those same hiding places create that same sense of refuge – and a welcome that has been preserved for over 350 years.

'The King of England, my master, your master and the master of all good Englishmen, is near you and in great distress; can you help us?'

Lord Wilmot pleads for help during Charles's flight

Opposite View of the house from the Knot Garden

Right An oil painting of King Charles II as a young man, after Adriaen Hanneman, c.1601

# Mr Pitt's new hall at Moseley

**Mr Pitt was an ambitious man. He must have been, to build a house as striking as Moseley Old Hall.**

This timber-framed, Elizabethan farmhouse was built in around 1600 on the instruction of Henry Pitt, a Roman Catholic from the nearby parish of Bushbury. Henry was a 'merchant of the staple', a member of a corporation that dealt in British wool exports, which boomed in the 16th century. Part of the established mercantile class, Henry's position was one of local power and prestige. It is therefore no surprise that he built a house of such size and quality as Moseley, designed to display his status in a very public way.

## The ancient parish of Bushbury
The parish of Bushbury had been divided into manors since medieval times, with the families living in them also owning most of the land nearby, a mix of mainly sheep farms and woodland. It is perhaps hard to imagine today but, when Henry Pitt bought the land for his new house in 1583, Moseley was surrounded by quiet countryside; it stood close to the Royal Forest of Cannock Chase where, it was said, 'a squirrel could travel ten miles without touching the ground.'

## House proud

Despite its rural setting, Moseley was built in a highly prominent position. It stood on what was the main route from Wolverhampton to Stafford and, if its position was notable, so too was its design. The inside of Henry Pitt's house conforms to a typical 17th-century layout, yet its exuberant exterior sets it apart. Sadly, the house was encased in brick in the 1870s, but drawings, etchings and early photographs reveal its former, decorative look. Panels separated by beams were slotted close together, filled with wattle and daub and then faced with elaborate herringbone brickwork. While this sort of design was common on the façades of Elizabethan houses, Henry Pitt extended it to cover almost the entire exterior. Its windows, meanwhile, held latticed panes of glass, a rarity in homes of the period, making Moseley distinctive if not distinguished.

This architectural exuberance was perhaps a sign of the times. Under the reign of Elizabeth I, England had experienced a prolonged period of political stability and economic growth. This so-called Golden Age ushered in both prosperity and social change – even, in Elizabeth's early reign at least, for Roman Catholic families. The merchant class began to expand and flouted the strict rules designed to enforce the Tudor social hierarchy, using their decadence to signal their newly elevated social position.

Opposite Watercolour painting of Moseley Old Hall, illustrating the original timber frame visible from the outside of the house

## A Catholic home

As a Roman Catholic household, it's likely that the residents of Moseley were persecuted for their beliefs. During Elizabeth I's reign it became illegal to practise the religion, while to 'willingly receive, relieve, comfort, aid, or maintain' *(Act Against Jesuits and Seminarists,* 1585) a Roman Catholic priest was treasonable. Yet many wealthy families remained loyal to their faith, devising ingenious ways of concealing religious objects and even priests when necessary. It is clear that the hiding place used by Charles II at Moseley in 1651 was integrated into the structural design when the house was built.

**Charles II's many hiding places**
In the weeks following the Battle of Worcester, Charles II hid in five Roman Catholic houses equipped with hides. The hide at Boscobel House had been used only a week or so earlier by the Earl of Derby, but the hide at the house of Mr Woolf of Madeley, where Charles sought sanctuary during his attempt to reach Wales, had previously been discovered by soldiers. Mr Woolf was the head of another Roman Catholic family, but his brush with Cromwell's men made him reluctant to offer shelter – Charles's companion, Richard Penderel, was forced to disclose the true identity of the man with him before Mr Woolf would let the pair hide in his barn.

# The Whitgreaves of Moseley

**The story of Moseley Old Hall is almost entirely bound up with one family: the Whitgreaves. This influential, landowning family acquired Moseley and looked after it for over 200 years. As the Whitgreaves came to define Moseley, the story of Moseley Old Hall has come to define them.**

### The early Whitgreaves

It was Thomas Whitgreave (1568–1626), a Protestant Royalist, who first brought the Whitgreaves to Moseley Old Hall. He married the wealthy, widowed Alice Shaw, who inherited the house from her father, Henry Pitt. As a Roman Catholic, Alice was determined not only to retain her faith, but also to bring up her children in it.

### Alice Whitgreave (1580–1668)

The mother of eight children, Alice Whitgreave appears to have been a woman of substance. She flouted the laws that required her attendance at Church of England services and, as a result, faced heavy fines and the seizure of her estate in 1646 by Parliament (it was only after the restoration in 1660 that it was fully reinstated to her). When Thomas died, she managed the Whitgreave estate herself. In 1651, as the remnants of King Charles II's defeated army straggled its way past Moseley Old Hall, she tended to their wounds. She gave refuge to a stranger – who she would only later discover was Charles II – in his hour of need, despite facing the ultimate penalty should he be discovered.

### Thomas 'the Preserver' Whitgreave (1618–1702)

Thomas and Alice's son was named after his father, and he took his mother's Roman Catholic faith. In 1651, he was the only one of eight children still living at Moseley. He trained as a lawyer but is unlikely ever to have practised. Roman Catholics were barred from public office at the time. He was also a known Royalist, having fought for King Charles I at the Battle of Naseby, and would undoubtedly have been on the field at Worcester had illness not prevented him. It was perhaps as well he wasn't; it was Thomas who agreed to let Charles shelter at Moseley after fleeing the battlefield. He would later be remembered as Thomas 'the Preserver' for his courage and loyalty.

### Father Huddleston (1609–1698)

Although Father Huddleston wasn't a member of the Whitgreave family, he was instrumental in the King's escape. He was their resident priest, although his identity was kept secret – for anyone outside the family, he was simply known as 'Mr Huddleston', tutor to Thomas Whitgreave's two nephews and the young Sir John Preston, a boy in Huddleston's care at the time.

### The risks for Roman Catholics

Life for Roman Catholics in England had become increasingly difficult since Elizabeth I issued an Act for restraining Popish recusants in 1593. From that point, Roman Catholics found themselves barred from public office, forbidden to travel more than five miles without permission and required to attend Church of England services. If they refused, they were fined. If they didn't pay, their goods and estates were seized. Things got worse for families such as the Whitgreaves after the Civil War, with Royalist supporters and Roman Catholics imprisoned or executed, and the families left behind faced with crippling debts.

Opposite  Photograph of Moseley Old Hall, c.1860

Above left  Portrait of Thomas Whitgreave as a young man, c.1640

Above right  19th-century portrait of the Whitgreave's resident priest, Father John Huddleston

# How the King came to Moseley

**It is the 3 September 1651. Parliamentarian forces are closing in on the town of Worcester.**

What's left of King Charles II's defeated forces are fleeing – among them Charles himself. At only 21, Charles is used to the battlefield; he fought alongside his father during the early stages of the Civil War. This is Charles's most perilous moment. Galloping towards the relative safety of the town, with the Parliamentarian soldiers 'who did breathe out nothing but his death and destruction' (Allan

Fea, *The Flight of the King*, 1897) close behind, he comes to a decision: to make a final stand. Those with him are aghast. With little time for debate they manage to convince the King of the importance of his survival. Somehow, despite Worcester being surrounded by Cromwell's cavalry and despite the best of the New Model Army baying for his blood, Charles II escapes the 'faithful city' through the last gate still open. So begins six weeks on the run, a journey during which the King will seek refuge at Moseley Old Hall.

Below  An engraving of the Battle of Worcester (1651) c.1800

## Little Rome

In the aftermath of the Civil War, it had never been more dangerous to declare for the royal cause and yet, as Charles rode out that night, it was such support that he desperately needed – and on which the future of the monarchy depended.

Charles rode north from Worcester with a group of 60 men that included Lord Wilmot, the Earl of Derby and Charles Giffard, a prominent Royalist from Staffordshire. They rode hard all day, reaching Kinver Heath, where the Earl of Derby suggested they spend the night at Boscobel House, Charles Giffard's hunting lodge on the Staffordshire border (now cared for by English Heritage). This was a last-minute change of plan as the dangers of his escape became clear. Once again the group changed their minds part of the way there, heading instead for the former Whiteladies priory – another Giffard house nearby and a more secluded one. By agreeing to head there, Charles had his first stroke of luck: he rode straight into a Roman Catholic stronghold.

In the 17th century, Staffordshire was home to many Roman Catholic families, and Wolverhampton was known as Little Rome because of the 'multitude of Papists' in the area.

## Whiteladies

The narrow, winding lanes and deep woodland that surrounded Whiteladies made for good cover; even so, when Charles arrived at dawn he was persuaded to disguise himself as a woodcutter, borrowing clothes and shoes, blackening his face with soot and cutting his hair. He was led to a coppice by Richard Penderel, one of the five brothers who lived nearby, and spent the day there before deciding that night to head west, to cross the River Severn and make for the safety of Wales. The decision to leave the house proved a good one: Parliamentarian soldiers arrived at Whiteladies less than half an hour after Charles had left for the woods.

Below The route Charles took in 1651 after the Battle of Worcester, which eventually led him to Moseley's front door and then southward on his journey to France via Bristol and Southampton

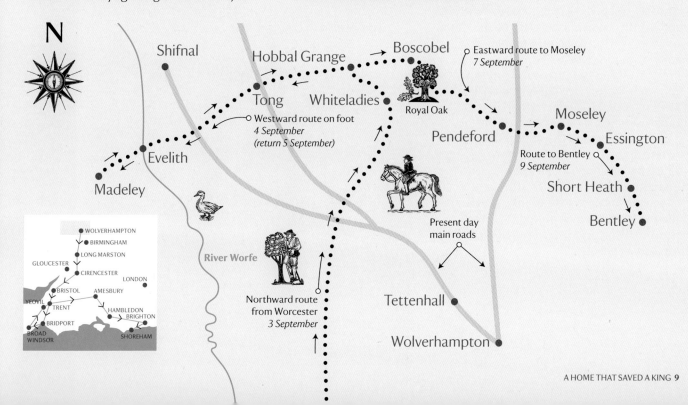

# A house that could keep its secrets

**The attempt to reach Wales was a disaster. After walking for miles disguised as a woodcutter, in shoes so small they cut into his feet, Charles and Richard Penderel found Parliamentarian soldiers blocking all crossings over the River Severn. With no way across the river, the pair had to make the long walk back to Boscobel.**

Rather than risk staying in the house, Charles again took refuge in the woods, climbing up an oak tree that would later be known as the 'Royal Oak', and again narrowly escaping arrest. Soldiers came so close to the tree that Charles could see troopers' helmets through the leaves, and Joan Penderel, mother of the five Penderel brothers, was forced to cause a diversion by gathering sticks close by.

While Charles had been walking west, the Penderels had found refuge for Lord Wilmot at Moseley Old Hall, enlisting the help of Father Huddleston and Thomas Whitgreave in the process. When they realised Charles had returned, they decided to bring him to Moseley. Under the cover of night on 7 September, Charles rode part of the way on the back of Humphrey Penderel's ancient mill horse, with the 'five faithful' Penderel brothers, armed with pistols, bill hooks and pikestaffs, forming a makeshift guard.

'My liege! Can you blame the horse to go heavily when he has the weight of three kingdoms on his back?'

Humphrey Penderel's reply when the King complained about his horse, the 'three kingdoms' referring to England and Wales, Scotland and Ireland

Carolus II D.G.M. Brit &c Rex

### The King's Door

Looking at Moseley's back door today, it is perhaps hard to imagine Charles standing here over 300 years ago. It made an impression on him, though: when Charles recalled his escape to diarist Samuel Pepys, he remembered enough of that night to give a description of the iron-studded door through which he hurried in the early hours of 8 September 1651. He described it as 'three planks wide and heavily studded'.

As for the inhabitants of Moseley Old Hall, the appearance of the King came as something of a shock. When Thomas Whitgreave greeted him, the King was so well disguised that Thomas only worked out who he was by a process of elimination – Charles was the only member of the party he hadn't previously met. Once inside, Charles hurried up the back stairs to Father Huddleston's room. Only Thomas, Alice and Father Huddleston were told his true identity – everyone else was simply informed that Moseley was sheltering a Royalist on the run from Worcester. It was just enough of the truth to seem plausible, without putting themselves and Charles at risk.

This page  The heavily studded back door of Moseley Old Hall, through which King Charles II entered in the early hours of 8 September 1651

Opposite  Engraving of Charles II on horseback, holding a baton in his right hand with the city of London seen between the horse's hooves c.1670

# Exploring Moseley

The exterior of Moseley Old Hall gives few clues as to its tumultuous past. Save for the star-shaped Elizabethan chimneys, there's little outside that King Charles II or the man of the house in 1651, Thomas Whitgreave, would recognise. Yet step inside and you are immediately transported back in time, to a period when all of England was in disarray, and when the young King faced the fight – and flight – of his life.

## A home through the ages

How did Moseley come to appear so different outside and in? While the house today is dressed to tell the story of the 17th-century Whitgreaves, like almost all homes of its great age it has been variously altered and enlarged, neglected and restored over its 400-year life. After Henry Pitt's original house-building efforts, Moseley appears to have remained relatively unchanged for the best part of a century. This lack of change perhaps isn't surprising. While the early Whitgreaves were influential, their wealth was dented by punitive fines, first for refusing to attend Church of England services and later, for their support of the monarchy.

In the 18th and 19th centuries the combination of political stability, a pension from the King and advantageous marriages resulted in a change in fortunes for the family. So it is from the Restoration of Charles II onwards where we begin to see these changes to the house. A new staircase was added in around 1713, then later in this period the second floor rooms above the Parlour were added and many rooms, such as the Main Hall and Parlour, were expensively panelled. The service wing was extended in the 18th century too. These rooms to the north side of the house were used by servants. They also appear to have been further enlarged during the 19th century. It was not until the Relieving Act of 1791, allowing a certain level of religious freedom for Roman Catholics, that the Chapel was lovingly decorated as seen today.

Left View of the house through the Front Garden in June

## Later decline

In around 1820 the Whitgreaves moved to the newly built Moseley Court, a fashionable Regency-style villa around half a mile away. Moseley – which then acquired the name Moseley 'Old' Hall – was let to a succession of tenant farmers and occupied by perhaps three families at a time. A series of partition walls carved up the Main Hall, the Staircase was enclosed and many of Moseley's interior oak panels were stripped and sold off. Without the Whitgreave family living in it, the house was neglected and, by 1870, some of its timbers were so badly rotten that they were taken out and the house encased in the brick skin we see today.

'There stood the house, a dull-array of blue-grey and reddish bricks; I had passed it twice, disbelieving that it could be the house I was looking for … There was the back gate through which Charles II entered from the fields in 1651, two days after the disastrous battle of Worcester. Since then the house had been encased in bricks, completely obscuring its beautiful half-timber work, but inside it is still much as the King would have seen it.'

Graham Stuart Thomas OBE,
*Gardens of the National Trust*, 1976

# The Kitchen

**This small room, with its red tiled floor, has had many uses over the years – from a kitchen to a makeshift brew-house – as the huge fireplace and grain chute reveal.**

The original hearth has long since disappeared, but visitors today can stand in this space, smelling freshly baked bread made using traditional methods, and get a sense of the home run by Alice and Thomas Whitgreave in the mid-1600s. It was here, in the early hours on the 8 September 1651, that the young Thomas Whitgreave ushered the Penderel brothers in for something to eat and drink, before their long, cold walk back to Boscobel.

## A self-sufficient household

Like most 17th-century homes, Moseley would have been largely self-sufficient. The family managed a farm, drew water from a well in the garden and produced much of their own food. A chute leading from the Attic directly down to the Kitchen fireplace – an efficient way of moving the malted grain stored there – illustrates one of the most important aspects of 17th-century domestic life: the making of beer. Rather than drink the often-contaminated water, households had beer, milk or wine – but mostly beer. Even children drank 'small beer', the final draught taken from a brew that was very weak.

Above left  Baskets of apples in the Kitchen

Below  A square, wooden Trencher plate

Above right  A bombard on the table in the Kitchen. They held eight pints of beer – the field workers' daily ration, hence the expression 'one over the eight' if someone is a little worse for wear

### Why do we say...

Many sayings used today have their roots in our domestic past, clues to which can be found all around Moseley Old Hall, especially in the Kitchen.

- *A square meal* – The Tudors ate from hard-baked square bread known as a 'Trencher'. By the time the King came to Moseley these were made of wood. When a good meal had been eaten, all that remained would be the square wooden trencher.
- *Cutting corners* – Tudor cooks realised they could get more pies for their pastry if they rounded the corners.
- *Power to your elbow* – You needed a strong elbow to drink from bombards and other vessels of the 17th century, as they would be rested on the forearm with a firm grasp on the handle.

# The King's Room and Hiding Place

**This room, once Father Huddleston's bedroom, was where Charles spent most of his time at Moseley. Close to Moseley's main hiding place and accessible via the back stairs, here Charles was able to rest, recover and formulate a plan for his escape.**

The room today contains the original four-poster bed on which the young King lay in 1651, fully clothed to aid a hasty escape – although for many years the bed wasn't at Moseley at all. It ended up in the hands of local politician and industrialist, Sir Geoffrey Mander, who lived at nearby Wightwick Manor (also National Trust) and took a keen interest Moseley. In 1962, Sir Geoffrey's widow, Rosalie Mander, gave the bed to the National Trust and it was moved back to its original home.

'He was a Romane Catholique, and I chose to trust them, because I knew they had hideing-holes for Preistes, that I thought I might make use of in case of neede.'

The King's narrative, as dictated to Samuel Pepys in 1680

Right   The King's Room

Far right   A cut-away watercolour sketch illustrating the Hiding Place off the King's Room, below a closet adjoining Father Huddleston's chamber

## Hiding Place

What made this room so special to Charles II was its Hiding Place. In the corner, next to the fireplace, is what was probably a wardrobe. Hidden in the floor is a trapdoor and, beneath that, the Hiding Place, capable of holding four people and whose door is secured on the underside with a stout wooden bolt. Through this cupboard, food could have been passed. Charles II declared this dark, cramped hiding place 'the best place hee was ever in'
– this witty remark at such a perilous time demonstrates the personality of the man who would later be known as the 'Merry Monarch'.

## The utmost secrecy

We know of at least one more hiding place at Moseley, a smaller one found behind a wall panel in the Garret, located in the Attic. There may have been others, but the existence of hides were usually known only to the owners and their priest; experience had shown Roman Catholic families such as the Whitgreaves that servants were too easily bribed or intimidated into revealing their whereabouts.

# Mr Whitgreave's Room and Study

**Thomas Whitgreave's comfortably decorated room, with its polished oak floorboards and panelling, gives us an insight into the life and status of a 17th-century merchant and his family.**

The portraits here help tell the story of Charles II and the Whitgreaves, with that of Thomas 'the Preserver' hanging over the fireplace. Painted in 1640, this portrait shows him at 23, a qualified lawyer – destined never to practise – and a man of utter conviction. Two years later, in 1642, Thomas would be at war, fighting under Charles Giffard, the man who would lead Charles from danger following the Battle of Worcester to Staffordshire. The oak spice cabinet is an indication of the family's status – its compartments used for storing the expensive, imported spices commonly used to flavour sweet and savoury dishes, and as a staple in home remedies.

Left  Spectacles resting on a book and feather quills on Mr Whitgreave's desk in his private Study

Above  Mr Whitgreave's Room, with his portrait as a young man hanging above the fireplace

Above right  Charles, James and Mary, Charles I's eldest children, painted by Sir Anthony Van Dyck (1635)

### The Royal children

On the wall also hangs an 18th-century copy of Van Dyck's portrait of King Charles I's eldest children. Mary was described as a 'terrible fidget' by her mother, frustrated by a little girl unable to stay still for the Flemish master. This flash of detail makes it easy to imagine Charles, James and Mary as lively, ordinary children. Their futures were to prove extraordinary, however, with their father executed in 1649, Charles II dying without a legitimate heir (although plenty of illegitimate ones) and his brother, James II, replaced by his own daughter in the 'Glorious Revolution' of 1688.

### The Study

A door in the panelling opens onto a small room, Thomas's study, which sits over the main porch. With both inner and outer doors, this was a private space where Thomas would have written confidential papers and discussed private matters. It was from here that Charles and Father Huddleston watched, in dismay, as stragglers from the King's defeated army made their way along the main route from Wolverhampton to Stafford on their long walk back to Scotland. With soldiers arriving barefoot, injured and half-starved, Alice Whitgreave took pity on them, dressing their wounds and offering much-needed food.

### Soldiers are coming!

Getting on with your neighbours is always a wise move, but perhaps more so when the country is violently divided by politics, religion and war. On the King's second day in the house, a neighbour came running to the door with news that soldiers were on their way. A servant then ran up the stairs shouting, 'Soldiers! Soldiers are coming!' Charles II made for the priest hole; Thomas Whitgreave left 'open all the Chamber dores' (Thomas Blount, Boscobel, 1651) so as to make it look as if he had nothing to hide and then went down into the courtyard (now the Front Garden) to meet the soldiers. It was a brave move. The soldiers accused him of having fought at Worcester, and were about to 'pull mee in peeces' when Thomas's neighbours again stepped in, confirming that he'd been at home, too ill to fight. Almost unbelievably, the militia left without searching the house, though not before a soldier called Southall the Priest-Catcher offered a blacksmith working in the yard £1,000 if he could tell them where the King was. As the smith knew nothing of the King's whereabouts, he was unable to betray him. Thomas, meanwhile, followed the soldiers almost all the way to Wolverhampton, to be sure that they wouldn't return.

**Why do we say...**
* *Sitting on your assets* – The chair table in this room has a concealed, lockable compartment – the perfect place to keep important documents pertaining to your property.

# The Attic

**Walk up the stairs to the top of the house and the atmosphere changes. Gone are the polished floors and panelled walls. Unfinished timber protrudes and the huge, five-flue chimneystack dominates. It is here that you can get closest to the original Elizabethan building, and to the timber frame that could once be seen not just inside, but outside, too.**

## The Garret

This small room, which sits directly above Thomas Whitgreave's Study, offers an unimpeded view of the main road. It was here that Father Huddleston's three pupils were stationed during Charles II's stay, where they were told to keep watch 'and give notice when they saw any Troopers' (Thomas Blount, *Boscobel*, 1660). For two days, the boys did so diligently, running quietly down the back stairs to alert Father Huddleston when they saw strangers approach. There is another hiding place above this tiny room, its diamond-shaped opening covered by a whitewashed trapdoor, which may have been the space where liturgical objects for conducting the mass were kept.

'Eat hard boys, for we have been on the life guard and hard duty this day.'

> The young Sir John Preston speaking to Thomas Whitgreave's two nephews at supper, after spending the day on watch at the Attic window

**Why do we say...**
* *Top dog and underdog* – The large saw pit where timber would be cut for the community would be straddled by beams and held in place at each end by dog irons. If a large timber was being cut along the length of the pit, the man on top guiding the saw was the 'top dog' while the man underneath was the 'underdog'.

## Typical Tudor house building

Beneath its brick exterior, Moseley is a typical timber-framed, Tudor house. A central hall is flanked on one side with a 'parlour wing' (where the family lived and entertained) and a more functional service wing on the other (where Charles first came into the house). Most timber-framed buildings of that period were made in a similar way; a series of pre-made posts and beams slotted together on site and placed on stone footings, the panels formed by each part of the frame filled with willow and hazel wattle, covered with daub, a mixture of mud, muck and straw, and finally lime washed. Some of the original wattle and daub is still visible in the Attic. During building works, it's likely that the house was raised one floor at a time – walls, floors, even chimneys and staircases. The intricately made scale model of Moseley shows the building process.

Left Dry herbs hanging in the Garret

Below Miniature model of Moseley Old Hall

# The Chapel,
# The Ante-room,
# The Bedroom

### The Chapel

The Chapel was a place of great secrecy, a plain space where nothing was left out that might betray its use – the vessels, books and vestments used during Mass had their own hiding place. The barrel-vaulted ceiling, and the blue and gold star decoration above the altar, were both added after the Roman Catholic Relief Act of 1791, when worship in England became legal for the first time in almost 200 years. The beautiful, 17th-century Spanish crucifix that once belonged to the Whitgreaves wasn't in use during Charles II's visit; it was donated by John Lockley Joseph Whitgreave in the mid-20th century.

'His Majestie wisht Mr Huddleston to show him our oratory, saying hee knew hee was a priest and hee needed not fear to own itt to him. For if itt pleased God to restore him to his kingdom wee should never need more privacies.'

Thomas Whitgreave and
John Huddleston's account
of the King's visit

Far right  The Derbyshire patterned chairs either side of the Altar are thought to represent Charles I and Charles II: one has a sad face with a pointed beard carved on the back, the other a smiling face

Right  Altar in the Chapel

## Charles visits the Chapel

Charles and Father Huddleston became close during the King's short stay, with Charles asking the priest to show him the Chapel. He described the simple room as a 'very decent place', and pledged then that if he ever regained his throne he'd see to it that Roman Catholics wouldn't have to worship in secret. In truth, Charles had little success. Although he married a Roman Catholic, Catherine of Braganza, he chose to profess a moderate Protestant faith. His Royal Declaration of Indulgence was an attempt, in 1672, to revoke the penal laws in place against Roman Catholics, but it was rejected and instead replaced by a set of even harsher laws. It would be a further 100 years before Roman Catholics would be able to openly practise their faith in England. Charles, however, never forgot his time with Father Huddleston. As his brother James II recalled, when the King lay dying, an elderly Father Huddleston was brought to him. James greeted him with the words: 'This man who once saved your body has now come to save your soul.'

## The Ante-room and Bedroom

The Whitgreaves' Chapel was not for their sole use. Other Roman Catholic families would come to worship here and the narrow Ante-room was probably used as an overspill, with the oak doors of the Chapel folded back during particularly busy services. The small room at the front of the house appears to have had several uses, perhaps once as a servant's bedroom. The acorn decoration carved into the bed frame refers to the famed episode of Charles hiding in an oak tree and is known as a 'Restoration bed'.

---

### Why do we say...

- *Crossing the threshold* – Thresh was a mixture of herbs and reeds used to cover floors, helping to keep them warm and add a sweeter smell in the room. The wooden bar across the door at floor level was designed to hold the threshings in place.

- *Goodnight, sleep tight, don't let the bedbugs bite* – Truckle beds were common in the 16th and 17th centuries. They were stored under the main bed and pulled out at night for children or servants to sleep on. Mattresses varied, tending to be stuffed with whatever material was available (wool, feathers, rags and even moss); these were stacked on top of a straw one, with ropes beneath pulled tight using a thick wooden wedge known as a 'bed bug' for comfort.

# The corridor and staircase

**The danger to those who helped the King after the Battle of Worcester can't be underestimated; nor can the sense of danger and tumult into which England descended. On the walls in the corridor hang several original documents that illustrate this period of such turmoil.**

## The Proclamations

The hastily printed documents show the highly efficient and totalitarian regime that moved to quash any support for the King and his cause. They are pieces of propaganda produced and issued by the Commonwealth of England in 1651. One warns against corresponding 'with Charles Stuart or his party' and sets out the penalty for doing so: charges of treason. The other was distributed on 10 September 1651, after Charles had already left Moseley and as Cromwell's forces scrambled to cement their victory at Worcester. It offers a reward of £1,000, more than an average man could earn in a lifetime, for the capture of 'Charles Stuart Traytor' – and was printed and packed so quickly that the smudged imprint from the wet copy that sat below this one is still visible.

Right  Proclamation declaring Charles Stuart and his party to be traitors

Far right  The spiralling wooden staircase

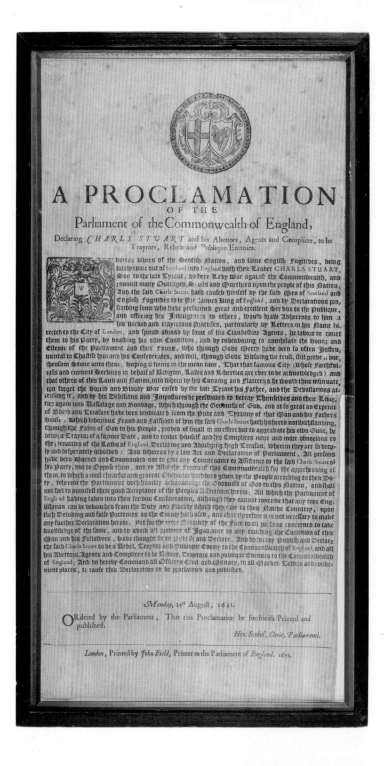

## The staircase

The chaos of the Civil War did eventually subside, and life for families such as the Whitgreaves settled down. This wide, graceful staircase was probably installed around 1713 by Thomas 'the Preserver's' son. Hanging nearby are the two original Royal Warrants for the Whitgreave pensions, the second noting that the pension was to be extended to Thomas Whitgreave's son, Thomas – doubtless this extra money helped finance the new staircase and other improvements. Much later, the staircase was enclosed to prevent draughts and the hall downstairs divided by a partition; restoration in the 1940s stripped both back to reveal a stair and hall that are closer to that which the 17th and 18th-century Whitgreaves knew.

### The gift that keeps on giving

Some of the financial gifts bestowed by Charles still exist today. The Penderel Grant, 1675, was a gift of £100 to four of the Penderel brothers and a pension for all five Penderel brothers paid to them and their heirs thereafter. The Penderel Trust continues to make payments to the Penderel descendants to this day. The present-day owner of Chillington Hall and a descendant of Charles Giffard, Mr John Giffard, is one of the pension's trustees.

# The Main Hall

**This was one of the finest rooms in the Whitgreave's 17th-century house, a grand open space fit for entertaining, feasting and organising a household.**

The Hall was a central place for the household to gather, the heart of family life, its walls probably covered with oak panels as a statement of wealth and status. The furniture today is from the period. The dining table is around 400 years old, while the gloriously carved livery cupboard – used for storing food between courses – dates to the late 17th century. Note the lantern clock.

The fact that it only has a single hour hand makes it unusual to our eyes, yet before the late 1650s English clocks were almost all produced this way. People worked, ate and slept depending on sunrise and sunset – minutes didn't matter.

While the Hall served as the main entrance to the house, and thus was suitably grand, it was also a practical space. Food was eaten with the family and servants sharing most of their meals at a long wooden table, each person's place set out according to a strict hierarchy. Social status and hierarchies were enforced through where you sat and the food you were served.

Above  The Main Hall with a fire burning in the fireplace

Right  Rushlight holder above the fireplace

## Why do we say...

● *Burning the candle at both ends* – The iron holders on the fireplace once held rushlights, a type of candle made by soaking the dried pith of the rush plant in animal fat and allowing it to harden. If extra light was needed, the rushlight would be lit at both ends.

● *Worth your salt* – The salt cellar was carefully placed on the table depending on who was coming to dinner. Those placed above the salt were higher in the social ranking, and so worthy of the highly valuable Tudor seasoning.

● *Turning the tables* – In this period the main table consisted of a frame and detachable board and has inspired many sayings and expressions. This board was rough on one side, where meals would be taken, and smooth and polished on the other, for display *(you take the rough with the smooth)*. They were often removed to form a makeshift bed for visitors, hence *bed and board*. The head of the household was the only one to sit in a chair with arms, and so he was known as the *Chairman of the Board*. If he held a meeting with servants or estate workers, they all sat round for a *board meeting* and, if gaming or gambling was allowed, the players would be expected to keep their hands in view, thus staying *above board*.

# The Parlour

**This private but sumptuous space was perhaps the best room in the house, an intimate space open only to the family and their most important guests.**

At the front of the house, lit by two large windows, the Parlour expressed to all who saw it that the Whitgreaves were a family of some wealth and local importance. The walls were panelled on all sides, and the room filled with fine furniture and china. Carpets were displayed on tables rather than floors, as woven and decorative fabrics were very precious and a sign of status.

The design carved into the lower doors of the court cupboard is similar to that of the frieze over the wall panelling: this suggests it was bespoke, made locally for the family. Often patterns in all forms of decoration were typical of the individual craftsman or area of production.

'It is impossible I can ever forget the great debte I owe you, whch I hope I shall live to pay, in a degree that is worthy of me.'

King Charles II writing to Jane Lane after his safe arrival in France, 1652

Above right  The Parlour at Moseley Old Hall

Opposite  Letter from Charles II to Jane Lane, thanking her for her assistance in his escape to France

## Risks and rewards

Some of the portraits in this room are of the characters who played a part in the next stage of Charles's story after he left Moseley: Father Huddleston, Jane Lane, Colonel John Lane and the King himself (copied from a Van Dyck original in the 1820s). They are a visual reminder of the tight-knit community of Royalist families who put their own lives at risk in order to aid the King's escape. There is a happy ending to this tale. Almost nine years after fleeing England, Charles II returned and was reinstated as King. He did not forget those who had helped him. Thomas Whitgreave, Charles Giffard, the Penderels, Father Huddleston, Jane Lane and Colonel Lane (who was newly released from prison) were all granted pensions. Father Huddleston was granted immunity from religious persecution and became chaplain to Henrietta Maria and then to Catherine of Braganza, Charles II's Roman Catholic wife and Queen. He was the only Englishman allowed such an office.

## Letter to Jane

In a letter dated 23 November 1652, written in the King's own hand from the safety of Paris, Charles II writes to her as his 'most affectionate friend', Jane Lane. In it, he tells her that he hopes to live long enough to repay the enormous debt he owes her. There is no doubt that it was written by Charles: the paper bears both an official French watermark of the period and the King's seal. At the time the letter was sent, both Charles and Jane were safely on the continent. For many Royalists who could escape, exile was safer than remaining in England. It would not be until 1660 and the Restoration when England would return to relative peace and prosperity after the troubled times of the Civil War and the Commonwealth.

M:rs Lane, I haue hither to deferred writing to
in hope to be able to send you some what else be[?]
a letter, and I beleeue it troubles me more, that
cannot yett doe it, then it does you, though I a[m]
not take you to be in a good condition longe to e[x]
=pect it, the truth is, my necessityes are greater [than]
can be imagined, but I am promised they shall
shortly supplyed, if they are you shall be sure
receaue a share, for it is impossible I can euer fo[rget]
the great debte I owe you, w:ch I hope I shall [liue]
to pray, in a degree that is worthy of me, in the m[ean]
time I am sure all who loue me will be very kin[d to]
you, else I shall neuer thinke them so, to,

Your most affectiona[te]
frind

Charles R

Paris Nou: 23.
1652.

# The Flight from Moseley

'I changed my Cloathes into a little better habitt like a Serveing-man, being a kinde of grey Cloathe suit; and the next day Mrs Lane and I tooke our journey towards Bristoll.'

King Charles II describes the disguise he wore on his journey south

Jane Lane was the sister of Colonel John Lane, both of whom were from a known Protestant, Royalist family and living at Bentley Hall, four miles away from Moseley.

During the Civil War it was illegal for all non-Commonwealth supporters to travel more than five miles from their homes without permission, but some time before the Battle of Worcester Jane had managed to get a permit to visit her heavily pregnant friend in Bristol. During the King's time at Moseley it was decided that he would ride with her, disguised as her servant, across 100 or so miles of countryside to reach the city. It was undoubtedly a risky journey – both would have been executed had they been caught. As with the story of the Royal Oak, when the story became public it lit a fire within England's collective imagination. Although Jane didn't write her own account of what happened, countless ballads and popular 17th-century songs filled in the gaps. Fortunately, Charles and Jane's audacious and improvised journey to Bristol worked. Unable to set sail from Bristol, Charles travelled from there over a period of five weeks on to Shoreham, where he was finally able to find a boat to take him to safety in France.

Right Painting of Jane Lane who aided Charles II's escape to France

Below King Charles II making his escape in disguise, riding before Jane Lane

## Not all saviours could be saved

The story of Charles II's escape was kept a closely guarded secret to protect those involved. While in exile in France, Charles told several versions of the story (one had him escaping via Scotland) to throw people off the scent. Even so, several of those involved were caught, including Francis Yates and the Earl of Derby, who were both executed. Charles Giffard, Jane Lane and Colonel Lane fled the country; Giffard and the Colonel later returned and were thrown in prison. The day after the King left Boscobel, soldiers ransacked nearby Whiteladies. Bentley Hall was also plundered. As for Thomas and Father Huddleston, they left Moseley and returned only when they were sure that Charles was safe and their part in his escape was unknown; leaving Thomas's mother, Alice, to run the household and take charge of Moseley in these troubled times.

# The Gardens

The gardens at Moseley are perhaps best described as an illusion. With its Knot Garden and period-appropriate plants – everything from heritage apples to cottage-garden flowers – it appears to be every inch Thomas Whitgreave's work. Yet nothing here is original. The garden is an historic recreation, one of the first of its kind, undertaken by the National Trust in the early 1960s.

By the mid-20th century, the land immediately around the house was largely empty, devoid of any planting. The Trust therefore turned to the renowned horticulturalist Graham Stuart Thomas OBE. He began working informally with the Trust in 1948, and later acted as its official gardens advisor. It was Thomas who designed these gardens in 1962, using plants that were known to be in gardens before 1700, which has set the principal of planting at Moseley ever since. The gardens reveal Thomas's extensive horticultural knowledge of the period, as well as careful consideration of setting, creating a garden that is both historically apt and quietly beautiful.

**Left** The garden at Moseley Old Hall

**Below left** View through the Orchard, with one of the bee boles set into the wall

## The Herb Garden and Kitchen Garden

The Herb Garden is modest in size but it contains a wide variety of herbs reflecting their importance in 17th-century life. They were used in Tudor and Stuart cooking – for flavour, preservation or the making of medicines and home remedies. Growing here are plants such as golden marjoram, mace, chamomile, thyme and comfrey. You can also find Good King Henry (*Chenopodium bonus-henricus*), a kitchen garden staple whose tender stems can be steamed and eaten and whose leaves were often included in elaborate 'sallats' – or salads – enjoyed as the 17th century progressed. These would often feature lettuce, borage and Good King Henry leaves, as well as myriad herbs, such as the rue and skirret grown in the Herb Garden, nuts and edible flowers (such as rosemary flowers). The salad would be dressed in a way we would recognise today: with a dressing made from oil and salt.

'And of the garden ... Apart from a few wind-bitten yews and a few old fruit trees, a variegated holly and an old pear growing up the south wall, there was nothing. Nothing, that is, except the old surrounding walls, some pig sties, hen-coops and broken glass cloches ... the resolve was to create one such as he (the King) might have seen.'

Graham Stuart Thomas OBE,
*Gardens of the National Trust*, 1979

### Why do we say...

● *Frog in the throat* – In medieval times one of the old folk cures for a sore throat or a cough was to dangle a little yellow frog head first into the throat. The frog would give out some stringy saliva, which the patient had to swallow slowly. The frog would often struggle and its feet might aggravate the soreness, and so making the patient hoarse.

### Home remedies

The Whitgreave's garden was an essential part of their self-sufficient household, and the Herb Garden provided not just food and flavourings, but medicine, too. To our eyes, 17th-century medicines may seem bizarre: a glass of wine mixed with crushed woodlice to treat asthma, for example, or powdered hen's dung for sore eyes (the patient would have to endure the pungent dust being blown into their eyes). Even more serious conditions were 'treated' with remedies such as these. The cure for an adder bite was a mixture of mashed nuts, rue, garlic and treacle, swirled together in a glass of beer, while a recipe for 'Plague Water' consisted of rue, rosemary, sage, sorrel, celandine, mugwort, angelica and 'the tops of red brambles' steeped in white wine. However, since the Middle Ages, plants and their uses were well understood and the practice of herbal cures well established and often effective.

# The Front Garden and Knot Garden

**In Thomas Whitgreave's time, this peaceful spot was a more functional space, either a cobbled courtyard or a saddling yard that Father Huddleston referred to as the 'equipage'.**

## The Front Garden

Today, the cobbled path leading to the front door is bordered by a low germander hedge *(Teucrium chamaedrys)*; an ancient medicinal plant used for the treatment of gout, but one that is also highly decorative. Its long-lasting blooms are alive with bees during the summer and autumn months.

The Front Garden is sheltered, even on windy days, enabling the creation of year-round colour and interest. There are roses known and grown in Stuart times, such as the Red Rose of Lancaster *(Rosa gallica officinalis)*, the Jacobite Rose *(Rosa alba maxima)*, and the Eglantine or Sweet Briar *(Rosa eglanteria)*. The herbaceous borders feature a double form of the soapwort *(Saponaria officinalis)*, used for cleaning fabrics, red valerian *(Centranthus ruber)*, pink and red peony *(Paeonia officinalis)* and Cupid's dart *(Catananche caerulea)*, the latter once an ingredient in love potions. And there are bulbs, too, in the form of crown imperial fritillaria and martagon lilies.

**Left** View from the house of the Front Garden with the cobbled path leading to the gate at the edge of the garden

**Right** View of Moseley Old Hall from the Knot Garden

## The Knot Garden

The showpiece of Moseley Old Hall is the Knot Garden. There are no surviving Elizabethan knot gardens – they fell out of fashion during Charles II's reign – but original plans for them remain. The design of Moseley's is based on one of five laid out by the Rev Walter Stonehouse, Rector of Darfield in Yorkshire, in 1631. It is an 'open knot', with coloured gravel laid between sections of dwarf box hedge laid out in an interconnecting and symmetrical pattern (a closed knot typically has plants and flowers in place of gravel), and despite its intricate design it is relatively straightforward to maintain. Weeding the gravel and plant feed is all that is required, together with an annual trim that takes five people a week to complete.

### Why knot?

The word 'knot' first appears in a horticultural sense at the end of the 15th century, when gardens were inspired by contemporary needlework designs. The 'knot' was usually a small, rectangular bed upon which was outlined an intricate (or 'enknotted') pattern. These formal gardens were designed to look particularly attractive from inside the house, and one of the best places to view Moseley's is from the Attic Bedroom or Parlour.

# The Nut Walk and Orchard

**As with so much at Moseley, the gardens serve both an aesthetic and a practical purpose. While being pleasant to view from inside the house, the gardens would have always been a place of production, where fruits, herbs and vegetables would have been grown.**

## The Nut Walk

The Nut Walk is one such example. The hazel trees that line either side of the path create a long arbour through which the Knot Garden can be glimpsed, while the bulbs planted beneath poke through the grass, and splashes of colour come from snowdrops, cyclamen, a few winter aconite, snake's head fritillary and meadow saffron. It is an appealing sight; the trees produce either the common hazelnut (also known as a cobnut) or the slightly longer filbert nut. The flagstone path that leads back to the house is flanked by quince, mulberry and medlar trees. In the far corner of the walled garden, at the end of the walk, is the gateway through which Charles II quietly stole; it leads on to an area of woodland shown on some historic maps as King's Walk Wood, and is believed to be the direction Charles walked here from Boscobel.

Right Bench seat among hazel trees in the garden

## The Orchard

This small orchard is stocked with fruit trees that were common in the 17th century. Most of them were planted in the decades after the National Trust took over ownership of the house. They include a London pippin, which dates from 1580, and the catshead cooking apple that can be traced back to 1629. Its name is derived from the distinctive, square shape of a sharp fruit that makes it excellent for sauces and stewed apple. There is a Norfolk biffin which, slow baked, was a popular Victorian treat ('Biffin cakes' were usually eaten with sugar and cream). Other varieties include the peardrop-like flavour of the 16th-century nonpareil, the deep-red Devonshire quarrenden, and the ancient French dessert apple, the court pendu plat.

Above right  Fruit trees in blossom in the Orchard

Right  A bee bole in the Orchard wall

### Bee boles

Prior to the 18th century, when sugar imports rocketed and prices fell, refined sugar was still a rarity – so expensive and exotic that it was referred to as a fine spice or medicine. Every-day sweetness therefore came in the form of fruit and honey, and it was commonplace for large households such as Moseley to keep bees; not only for the production of honey, but also to pollinate the vast variety of fruit trees. The 'bee boles' are the alcoves built into the wall, with the basket or 'skep' effectively forming the 'hive'. They would be set into sheltered, sunny walls to help the hives survive the winter. Today Moseley has four modern hives in the field, which help support local bee populations.

### A pear as 'hard as bricks'

Moseley's apple and pear varieties are a reminder of how many have been lost, particularly those particular to specific locations. Take the Tettenhall dick, a small, dry pear that originated in a Wolverhampton suburb. The Black Country was once well known for its cider and perry, and this tough little pear was used for the latter and often sold with the cry, 'Tettenhall dicks are hard as bricks'. It fell out of favour in the latter half of the 20th century and, in a bid to save it, the charity Bees & Trees planted 2,000 Tettenhall dick trees across the Midlands – and the pear is now part of the National Fruit Collection at Brogdale and, of course, here at Moseley. The National Trust, meanwhile, is actively reintroducing rare and lost apple and pear varieties across the country in order to preserve and protect these rare species.

# King's Walk Wood

**The path through the garden gate traces the route that Charles II took as he made his approach from Boscobel to Moseley Old Hall in 1651.**

King's Walk Wood is a young wood planted in the last 100 to 150 years. Historic maps show that this area has come in and out of agricultural arable and pastoral use over many years. The oldest tree at Moseley can be found between the King's Walk Wood and the Orchard, a sweet chestnut thought to be between 250 and 300 years old. In recent years, the National Trust has gradually acquired more land around Moseley to shield it from the motorway and to improve biodiversity for nature. Native trees have been planted, acting as a screen, along with a wildflower meadow, with the aim of returning the land to a similar pastoral landscape as that in the 17th century – retaining a sense of shelter and calm, characteristic of Moseley Old Hall for over 400 years.

## The Tree Hide

The design of this fantastic tree hide was inspired by the story of Charles's journey of escape, hiding in an oak tree just before he took refuge within Moseley's walls. There is even an oak bed on the second floor where a tired king can take a rest while hiding from Cromwell's soldiers.

'People have flocked to see the royal oak, which has been deprived of all its boughs by the visitors of it, who keep them in memory of his Majesty's happy preservation.'

Thomas Blount, writing in 1651

### The tree that launched a thousand pubs

The story of the Royal Oak is irresistible (see page 10). Even before Charles's restoration, souvenir hunters began stripping the tree to make trinkets, while acorns pocketed at Boscobel were planted all across England. The tree inspired songs, village names, the innumerable Royal Oak pubs that still dot the country, and even a new public holiday. Oak Apple Day was celebrated on 29 May to commemorate Charles II's restoration and is still marked in some villages – and, of course, every year at Moseley. The original Royal Oak died before the end of the 17th century; the oak that stands at Boscobel House is a direct descendant and is thought to be over 300 years old.

Above  Peacock perched on the farmyard wall

Opposite  The Adventure Play Area in the King's Walk Wood

## The farm buildings

The farm buildings that surround Moseley Old Hall give a clue to the activities and work that continued here for centuries. In an area known for its sheep farming, this was the heart of a large working estate. The buildings were acquired by the National Trust in 1987 and restored for their current uses, including a large threshing barn, cowsheds, small stable and pigsty. They indicate the family's later prosperity, in particular the 18th-century coach house, which is currently used as a tea-room.

# Saving Moseley

## Despite its significance, Moseley Old Hall could so easily have been lost.

Although the Whitgreaves owned the house for over 300 years, by 1822 they had moved to Moseley Court, half a mile away.

Divided up into several dwellings, their former home was rented out, its Main Hall partitioned off and the original timber frame encased in brick. Little remained of the house that once welcomed Charles II.

It was saved thanks to the intervention of two local families and the National Trust, who have gradually restored it since 1962. Today, the National Trust preserves and protects one of the most remarkable homes in the long, tumultuous tale of the British monarchy – Moseley Old Hall.

### 'Old Hall' rescues the Old Hall

Moseley was sold to the Holly Bank Colliery in 1922, together with the mineral rights held since 1918 (as the house sits on coalfields beneath). With little investment and the threat of subsidence caused by mining, Moseley's future looked gloomy. By 1940 not all rooms were habitable, and the house was in dire need of structural repairs. Salvation came in the form of local manufacturer, J&J Wiggin. The company, which became renowned in the post-war years for its 'Old Hall'-branded tea and coffee sets, toast racks, cutlery and candlesticks, was at that time Britain's only manufacturer of stainless steel tableware, and highly successful as a result.

In 1940, its owner, William Wiggin, and his wife Nellie, bought Moseley Old Hall. Although their restoration plans were delayed first by the Second World War and then by the shortage of building materials thereafter, they did manage to restore the house sufficiently to open it to the public in the late 1940s, albeit only on Thursday afternoons. Their legacy would be the research, restoration and partial furnishing of the Hall, working to secure a future for a home with such an important past.

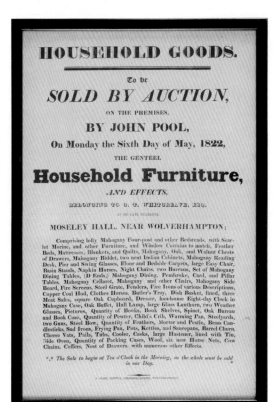

Left 1822 poster advertising an auction for apartments that had been created within Moseley Old Hall following the Whitgreaves' move to Moseley Court

Opposite Watercolour of the Attic (aka the Old Cheese-room), illustrating the exposed beams and brickwork by W.Wiggin, c.1947

'Mr and Mrs Wiggin have done far more than would have been thought possible to restore the homeliness of the 17th and 18th centuries and to bring back to the country, this great historical mansion with its air of friendliness and loyalty.'

*Staffordshire Life,* May 1949

This page : Photograph of
Moseley Old Hall, c.1958

Right Anthea Mandler
visiting Moseley with her
father, Geoffrey Mandler

# Making the case for Moseley

**Moseley Old Hall, however, needed more attention than the Wiggins could afford. A management committee was put together; two of the trustees were Roy Chand, a prominent local physician, and Sir Geoffrey Mander, a local industrialist and MP.**

## The Chands

Roy Chand and his wife May worked tirelessly to promote the importance of Moseley Old Hall and his work for the National Trust earned him an MBE in 1980. He was Secretary of the Moseley Old Hall Management Committee from 1961 until the Trust took over in 1962. In later years, he and May volunteered as guides at both Moseley and nearby Wightwick Manor.

## Sir Geoffrey Mander

Sir Geoffrey campaigned for Moseley's historic and cultural value to be recognised. His ambition was realised in 1953, when the house was listed Grade II and defined by English Heritage as 'an important building of more than special interest'. It was enough to secure Moseley's future and, in 1962, Moseley Old Hall and close to ten acres (four hectares) of land were transferred in perpetuity to the National Trust.

## Granville Squires

A less well-known but essential figure in the saving of Moseley is the historian, photographer and filmmaker Granville Squires. When the house was opened to the public in the 1940s, he was commissioned to write its very first guidebook. He appears to have accepted the commission enthusiastically, undertaking much of his own first-hand research and even digging about inside the house to make his own discoveries. It was Squires, for example, who excavated, by hand, the rubbish-filled grain chute that leads from the Attic down to the Kitchen.

'He was typical of a particular sort of English radical, a man of wealth and position who devoted himself to public service.'

Stephen Ponder on
Sir Geoffrey Mander, from
the Wightwick guidebook

# Moseley under the care of the Trust

**The house that was given to the National Trust in 1962 was but a shadow of the former Whitgreave home in which Charles II took refuge.**

Moseley had been stripped of its contents, the estate and surrounding farmland long since sold off. Almost everything you see in the house today has been donated through gifts, loans or bequests – including the original bed that Charles slept on, given to the Trust by Rosalie Mander, Sir Geoffrey's widow, in 1962. The Whitgreave family gave to the Wiggins several remarkable gifts which they generously donated to the Trust, items such as the 17th-century Spanish crucifix that can be found in the Chapel.

The Trust has also gradually acquired another four hectares (ten acres) of land around the house, as well as the farm buildings that are used by visitors today, and conserves both the house and the land for future generations. It has restocked and recreated the gardens with plants of the period. Inside the house, staff and volunteers bring to life the warmth and welcome that Moseley offered a young man in need in 1651 – and they provide a reminder that Moseley Old Hall is more than just an historic house. This, we should never forget, is much more than that. This is a home that saved a king.

Above  Vistors exploring the gardens at Moseley

Left  Costumed volunteer sweeping the cobbled path in the Front Garden